The Indoor Triathlete

The Indoor Triathlete

Be triathlon ready 365 days a year.

Bill Hammons

Hafta Books
Atlanta MMXI

ISBN 978-0-9831263-0-0
Library of Congress Control Number: 2010919360

Designed by Archie Delapaz
www.turtlebeachstudios.com

Photography by Atwell Photography
www.atwellphotography.com

Printed in the United States of America

To Arthur, Tony, Miles and those that I have coached.

The Indoor Triathlete
Be triathlon ready 365 days a year.

Introduction -The best athlete in your high school, twenty to forty years later.
Overview - Benefit of three activities.

Chapter One -Why indoors rather than outdoors.

> Lower your risk of injury.
> Save your money.
> Save your time.
> Better weather, facilities and equipment.
> Do more triathlons.

Chapter Two - Will outdoors be different? Yes, and what you can do.

> Learn to sight while swimming in the pool.
> Ride your bike once a week or month outdoors.
> Run/walk once a week outdoors.

Chapter Three - Choosing your club's location.

> Your club needs to be close.
> Think of cost per use.
> Time, time, time.
> Pool, bike, treadmills, weights, in that order.

Chapter Four —Swimming. The water is your key to recovery.

> The swim is the first and shortest event.
> It doesn't pay to be the fastest swimmer.
> Your goal is to swim with control and then speed.
> Walk in the pool even if you cannot swim now.
> Work on breathing. Good swimmers do.
> The big opposite, your weight centers at your chest, not hips.
> The two most common freestyle stroke problems.
> Your ten-minute warm up is all about breathing.
> The rest of the swim is learning and applying techniques.
> Positional and performance swim drills.
> Vary your strokes and stroke technique to vary the energy required.
> Your brain improves while swimming.
> Your ten minute cool down swim is all about recovery and breathing.
> Passing people in the first transition is a good sign.
> When you look forward to the swim, the program's goal is accomplished.

Chapter Five — Biking. The bike or spin class could be your best time spent.

Relative to the other two, this is where most time is spent.
If you are new or it has been a while, the first class will be the hardest.
Adjust your spin bike so it is comfortable.
Find four comfortable positions on the bike.
Drink and eat while riding indoors.
Enjoy the music. It's your road.
Spin so your heart does more work than your legs.
Spin for recovery.
Push for strength, like you wish you had an easier gear.
Learn to get low and out of the wind indoors.
Learn to ride high to take advantage of the wind.
In spin class or alone on the bike, be at your best.
Get off the bike hydrated, refueled and ready to run.
Compare bike placement to swimming and running.
Buy a road bike, not a triathlon bike. Or use your existing bike.

Chapter Six —Running. The treadmill is how you will measure your progress.

Your weekly time trial to measure your improvement.
Learn your pace from your weekly time trial.
Relative to the other two, you can always walk.
Get used to walking or running after biking.
"Float running" is to improve your running technique.
A long run at race distance, not at race speed.

Chapter Seven —Weightlifting. The transformation you want from weightlifting and stretching.

The weights will keep you toned and keep injury away from you.
Balanced strength prevents injuries.
Determine your core strength.
Extend your core strength to your arms and legs.
Don't even try to see how much you can lift.
Keep your weightlifting aerobic and varied.
Be patient with weightlifting.
Measure progress by your body's responses and core strength gains.
Be prepared to lift LESS weight on some days.
Five minutes off the floor to test your functional core strength.

Twenty to forty years after graduation, you can probably tell me who the best athlete in your high school was. You can probably also rattle off the top five or ten. Whenever there is a high school reunion, you usually hear someone asking whatever happened to so and so.

Time changes our perspectives. The people who were the top athletes in your high school may not be the top athletes now. Some may have already passed away. Would you be interested in being one of the top athletes in your high school, twenty to forty years later?

At a swim workshop for triathletes, a group was sharing their goals beforehand. One person, who was already established, wanted to win an upcoming triathlon. Another person, almost as competitive and years older, wanted to be the first in her age group in that same triathlon. Yet, a memorable moment came when a doctor said that his long-term goal was "to be the only one in my age group."

Your goal, I hope, is to get into shape and be healthy for the rest of your life. If you can swim, bike and run, you will be in position to do whatever else you want to do.

Overview — The benefit of three activities.

A benefit that you will discover doing three activities is that you reduce your risk of injury. Overuse injuries account for more athletic injuries than any other reason. It's your nature to want to do a little more and a little more until something does hurt. If you fix your shin splints, then your hamstrings, knees, iliotibial band, or back are likely to hurt you next because you keep on pushing until something does hurt. If you have had a long athletic career in one sport, you probably have spent your career adjusting from one ache and pain to another.

This is less so with triathlon training. The training workload is spread across the body and is not solely focused on legs or upper body. You train yourself to move into the next activity before you are exhausted and injured.

If you happen to get injured and cannot do one of the three activities while training for a triathlon, you still can train in the other two, lift weights and stretch while avoiding further injury.

Doing three different activities, and varying body positions within those three activities, will keep you fresher mentally and physically. Triathlon training is a smart and healthy choice.

Lower your risk of injury.

You have probably fallen off your bike at some point in your life. Could you include a running injury and wondering if you were ever going to be able to swim back to shore?

Training outdoors is more risky. You have probably read about more than one cyclist or runner that was hit by a car. Just pounding the pavement, especially concrete, is an injury risk. After a great swim in the lake, you could cut your foot on something you did not see while walking to shore.

When you train indoors, you lower your risks and raise your consistency and odds of success. There are no boats or cars indoors. You probably won't have to wonder if it is light enough outdoors to workout. Your bike won't slip out from under you on gravel. Your gym probably even has a defibrillator hanging on the wall with trained personnel nearby. Not that I think you will need the defibrillator while training! The riskiest part to training indoors would be slipping on the pool deck. The most common injury would come from training too hard. If you can take care not to fall on the pool deck, I will do my best in this book to guide you to not over-train and hurt yourself while achieving your goal of being triathlon ready 365 days a year.

Save your money.

Training outdoors involves buying a bicycle and maybe more than one bike. Training outdoors also means buying clothing and equipment for the range of weather where you live.

It can cost quite a bit less for you indoors. There are many facilities with a pool, bikes and spin classes, treadmills and weights for $30–50 dollars a month. If you join a club, just ensure your contract gives you access to the facilities you need and let the club maintain the equipment and a clean environment. Let them maintain the pool. You will seldom have to oil or grease a bike or dry out your shoes after it rains. When you train daily indoors, think of how low your cost per use will be. Clubs make money by people not showing up and when you do show up, you will be making the most of your money invested.

Starting indoors also allows you to keep your costs lower while you are in the start up mode. You will find that you will initially need fewer clothes and less equipment indoors. For swimming you will need a suit and goggles. For riding, you will need a pair of cycling shoes and cycling or triathlon shorts to protect your feet and rear end. For running, you will need a good pair of running shoes. Any other clothing you can pretty much find at Walmart® with their Starter line of socks, shirts and shorts for about half the cost of brand name wear.

Save your time.

During a triathlon, you want to reduce your transition time. Indoor triathlon training saves transition time too. Indoors you can go from bike to treadmill to pool in a few minutes. It's hard to replicate that transition 150-200 times a year outdoors. Saving time and continued consistency in training will increase your odds of success.

Better weather and facilities.

You will find that working out indoors is healthier, even if cars did not exist. There are no potholes, speed bumps or curbs indoors. The water quality is regulated. You can ignore the air advisory warnings that some cities have. And best of all, your water and bathrooms are close by.

Training indoors can be very social if you want it to be and everyone has the same equipment, so no one is at a disadvantage there.

Do more triathlons.

When you train indoors, you will find that it is safer, cheaper, healthier, social, consistent and takes less time. You will do a swim, bike, and run every other day, and you will appreciate the convenience.

Consistency is key to your long-term success. Going indoors will mean that your environment/atmosphere will be more consistent. Your lighting will be more consistent. Your water temperature will also be more consistent year round. And yes, there will be days indoors where things are not perfect, so you might want to join a club with more than one location in town. Or have a friend at another club.

You may already be training outdoors from home and you know it is faster to leave the house running or biking and cut out the commute to the gym. You're right, it is faster to run or ride from your house. However, unless you have water for swimming, it will probably be faster to swim, bike and run from your gym. When you do two of the three from home and drive somewhere else for the water, you get away from the feeling of doing one event right after the other.

If your goal is to be as healthy as you can be, try training for a triathlon indoors. Doing 150-200 triathlons a year is a confidence builder.

Learn to sight and keep your arms in front of you while swimming in the pool.

The biggest change when swimming outdoors is that there are no lines on the bottom of the lake for you to follow. It is much harder to see when swimming outdoors because the water is murky. Just as you walk more slowly in a pitch black room, you will initially be disoriented swimming outdoors. You can prepare for this beforehand and learn to reorient yourself by swimming "blind" in the pool. And the good news is that you will be breathing more frequently to allow better vision. You will also be changing strokes often to be able to see more.

With the swim technique that I teach, you will always have an arm in front of you while swimming. Always having that arm in front of you while swimming in a murky lake gives you more confidence. Your anxiety about not being able to see will decrease. It's a similar experience to walking around in a pitch black room with your arms outstretched versus trying to navigate with your arms at your side. You will be more at ease with your arms leading your body when swimming outdoors.

Ride your bike once a week outdoors.

Bike handling is almost non-existent indoors. You will need to ride once a week outdoors to develop bike handling skills. Depending on your schedule, try to bike on the weekend during your long ride. You want to be comfortable steering, braking, shifting gears, turning corners, passing and being passed. Learning to handle a bike can only be done outdoors, yet once a week will suffice. Many bike riders don't touch their bikes for months and do just fine after a few miles back on the bike. So once you have experience handling a bike on the road, riding the bike outdoors again will not be an issue.

When I was a pure cyclist the main reason I fell off my bike was because I was tired and lost control. I was out of breath, fatigued and desperate to keep up with the pack. The fatigue impaired my judgment and made me more susceptible to crashing. Until Clair Young, the father of Olympians Roger and Sheila, pointed out the obvious to me, I did not realize what the real problem was. Clair said that "Fit riders are not hard on their bikes. It is the out of shape, tired rider that hits potholes, other riders and crashes."

Run/walk once a week outdoors.

Running or walking outdoors will probably be the easiest transition from indoors to outdoors for you. Running on the road will feel different initially. Yet after five to ten minutes your legs will adjust. Again, like cycling, if you can run outdoors once a week, you will be fine during the run in a triathlon.

Toss in a big hill when running outside for the experience. The treadmill cannot replicate running downhill and a long uphill that keeps going is different than adjusting your incline on the treadmill.

Your club needs to be close.

For some of you, this may be the shortest chapter. If you have one club or gym in town with a pool, that is your location.

If you have no club or gym with a pool, your plans will revolve around the closest water available.

If you live in an area with multiple clubs or gyms with pools, then you have more options. In some areas, there can be as many as three to five chains with one to two local options. If you do have more than one choice, think of the location before you sign the contract. You are signing a rental agreement. Here are some things to consider, because once you sign a contract it may take months before you're able to make any changes.

Consider location first. Which club is the closest time-wise? If you can get there in ten minutes or less, it's going to be hard to justify driving ten minutes further.

Consider location second. Which club has multiple locations? If the pool at location A is unavailable for two to three days, does the chain have another club in the area.

Consider location third. Does the club have out of town locations? If you travel, can you go to the clubs in other areas? For example, the YMCA has a Y AWAY program that allows you to workout at other participating Ys.

Think of cost per use.

There are two clubs where I work out and both have a low cost per use, although one costs $100 more a month. The more costly club comes with breakfast, towels and laundry service included. The more costly club is almost never busy. Expectation level is that I will have a pool lane, bike and treadmill to myself. Given all of the above, my cost per use is similar to my $30 a month membership at my second club.

If you only workout once per month, your cost per use will be unreasonable regardless of the club. Working out every day of the month means your cost per use could be in the range of one to four dollars a day.

The club's contract says a lot about the club's cost per use. Consider giving the club some credit if you can stop your membership with a month's notice. Some clubs also reduce the monthly fee if you are away for a long period. Also ask how much it costs to bring along a guest or family member.

Price for a club varies during the year. Many clubs have enrollment drives when they waive initiation fees or have lower monthly costs. Some reduce price when another member signs you up. Price can be negotiable. Considering your cost per use is more helpful than cost per month. Paying a dollar a day or four dollars a day may not be not as important as all the other factors.

Time, time, time.

Schedule. There are some twenty-four hour clubs. Most clubs operate on a 5AM-10PM M-F schedule. Weekend hours tend to be 8AM to 8PM. While it's a selling point to be open 24-7, does your schedule even allow you to work out after midnight?

The clubs internal schedule is also important to your plans. If there is an aqua aerobics class, the pool may be unavailable. If there is a spin class, it may fill up fast and a bike will be unavailable. If the club does not have enough treadmills, during its busiest hours, what would you do? Will you be training outside the club, rather than indoors, at the busiest times?

Pool, bike, treadmills and weights, in that order.

Cleanliness. Of course, the club must be clean enough for you. If the club is unappealing to you, move on because the current members and management seem to be living with it.

Because the Indoor Triathlete program will have you in the pool daily, the pool is your top priority.

You will also be spending the most time on the bike, which makes the bike your second priority. Any bike that you can adjust and find four comfortable positions fits the bill.

Third, is a decent treadmill that can go faster than you can go.

Weights or weight machines are the lowest of the three because you are just using weights for feedback on your easy days.

Fortunately, you can probably find a club with all four components much cheaper than doing it yourself at home. To create an equal home environment, you would be spending about twenty thousand dollars.

Bill demonstrates his thumbs up technique while rolling for breath of air. The hand position is shoulder friendly and turns the weakest part of the stroke into a strength.

Value good technique as much as a golfer, tennis player or baseball player would. Good technique is physically easier and requires less energy.

The swim is the first and the shortest event. It seldom pays to be the fastest in the water.

Time-wise, the swim is your shortest event. For a sprint triathlon, plan on a 10-15 minute swim, a 35-45 minute bike and a 25-35 minute run the first time you race. So your total time would be between an hour and fifteen minutes (1:15) to an hour and forty-five minutes (1:45). Your swim is only ten to fifteen minutes of that total time. Yet, you don't want that first ten to fifteen minutes of your race to be a watery purgatory.

Good swimmers, to increase speed, swim behind other good swimmers and "draft" off them in a triathlon or open water swim race. Drafting is following in the wake of the swimmer(s) in front of you. Just as it easier to draft behind a truck, car or another cyclist, so someone else breaks the headwind, you can draft in swimming. Drafting while swimming creates a ten to fifteen percent benefit to the swimmer directly behind. It's legal to follow a good swimmer when you can.

Whether you are right behind the first person out of the water or right behind the first person in your age group out of the water, you have "won" in my book. The race is far from over and you have positioned yourself right behind your competition. On the bike, in most triathlons, riders can't legally draft off another. And in the run, if your competitors are still just ahead of you doing the work of leading, you can mentally rest until you are ready to pass them. It seldom pays to lead someone else to the finish line where they can pass you.

Your goal is to swim with control and then speed.

For some people, the swim is the most out of control and upsetting ten to fifteen minutes of the race. People go off course and swim farther than needed. Goggle fogginess and leaks are common for beginners. Even if your swim technique is good, other swimmers might touch and kick you while you are swimming, which may bother you. There doesn't seem to be enough air as if you started a 5K run too fast. Swimming with control under these circumstances is your top priority.

Jim Stewart, national age group champion at several long distances, swims with control and speed. Jim has all of the physical characteristics that a top swimmer needs: height and shape for a potential cylindrical streamline and weight for momentum in between strokes. Yet what sets Jim apart is that he looks like he is swimming with more controlled "ease" than anyone else in the water. Jim can literally swim as fast as you can walk and make it look easier than walking. Jim Stewart achieves speed with control.

Walk in the pool even if you cannot swim now.

If you cannot swim, go to your pool and begin by walking and playing in the water. Get in and walk the time set aside for swimming in this program even if you cannot swim yet. It may take you a year to develop in your other two sports. Begin and spend that year gaining control in the water too. Put your face in the water and exhale out your nose if this is your first challenge. The same steps that children take in learning to swim, adults have to take too. There appears to be no skipping steps in the learning to swim process, unless you want to try the sink or swim approach (which is not recommended).

Work on breathing better. Good swimmers do.

The lack of air is the most common complaint about swimming. While watching the SEC collegiate conference championships, you might be surprised by how fast the swimmers in the five hundred meter race were breathing. They breathe every other stroke and not every third or fourth stroke. It's like watching a race for air. No one passes up the opportunity to get a breath. A five hundred yard swim is like racing a mile on the track. A five hundred yard swim is in the range of the four to six hundred yard swims that we often find in a sprint triathlon. The collegiate swimmers breathing every other stroke swim five hundred yards in four minutes and thirty seconds. If you swim five hundred yards in four minutes and thirty seconds in a triathlon, you could be three to five minutes ahead of most people after the swim. If breathing that often was good enough for collegiate champions and produced those results, it would be wise to breathe more often so that a lack of air is not your reason for slowing down.

If your brain is not getting enough oxygen, your judgment is impaired. Getting enough air to think clearly comes before anything else while swimming.

Achieving excellence at exhaling underwater is step one to breathing better. Surprisingly, there seems to be a carry over from childhood in seeing how long we can hold our breath underwater. Remember how you won if you could hold your breath longer than anyone else? Stop playing that game. The best exhale and inhale combination wins.

In CPR, the first thing you do is clear the airways. Make certain the "victim" can exhale. It doesn't do any good to inhale into lungs that are not clear and ready for air. In the same way, to inhale while swimming, you need to get good at clearing the used air out of the way through a long, powerful exhale. No exhale means no inhale.

The triathlon is an aerobic event and no matter how good a swimmer, cyclist or runner you are, you must always try to get better at exhaling to get better at breathing. Yes, some people do try to suppress the breathing so others don't realize how hard they are working. That could be a race tactic, yet it may not be a good training tactic. Frank Shorter and Emil Zatopeck were two gold medal Olympic distance runners who may have used breathing hard to break their competitors' rhythms. Shorter's and Zatopek's hard and heavy breathing was mentioned by many of their competitors after races. It may unnerve you too when someone passes you in a race exhaling harder than you.

The big opposite, your weight centers at your chest, not hips.

When coaching swimmers, the big opposite that people need to learn is to center their weight at their chest while swimming and not at their hips. On land you naturally center your weight at your hips, so you have a lot of experience and do it unconsciously. If you find yourself sinking in the water, it's because you are still trying to center your weight at your hips.

Your chest is your new center of balance in the water. If you want to swim easily and float all day, be on your upper chest or back. Being aware of where you center your weight is the first step. Being weight-centric over the chest, like breathing, is something that even the best swimmers work to improve. Novices can make rapid gains just knowing where their weight needs to center. And any time you start sinking or have to kick harder, you can tell immediately, it's because your weight shifted back to your hips.

The two most common freestyle stroke problems are:

One - Reaching over the water with your stroke.

Reaching underwater for a longer, streamlined stroke is good swimming. You can reach just as far underwater as you can above water and a benefit is that reaching underwater keeps your weight centered at your chest. Many swimmers "over stride" above the water with their swim stroke. They incorrectly keep their hands out of the water for the longest possible reach above the water. This is a mistake that moves the weight to your hips. It also takes your hand longer to arrive at where it needs to be to catch the water underneath you. Perhaps equally important, putting your arm stroke into the water at your shoulder creates a downhill incline, dropping your body's weight in that direction.

You get to choose the incline at which you swim. While you may think everyone is level in the water, there is plenty of film footage showing people swimming up an incline at the angle created by the arm above the water.

Like biking and running, you will want a slight downward incline while swimming. You create your downhill with your arms. You swim upwards when you reach up and forward over the water with your swim stroke. You create a downward incline with your arms when you get your stroke in by your shoulder and reach forward underwater. The benefit of creating a downward incline is that your weight falls forward as you swim. This will feel like a big exaggeration to take your arms from stroking up and forward to stroking down and forward.

Two - Bending your arms in front of you while swimming.

Arms bent in front of you while swimming can mislead you. Bent arms give the false perception of "good" effort, yet bent arms decrease your power, streamline and your stroke length. Like baseball, golf or tennis effort is secondary to placement. People tend to "drum beat" the swim stroke in front of the head because they feel more effort. That drum beat feeling is OK at your waist underneath you. Yet to have "drum beat" arms while placing the arms in the water in front of you is a no-no. Do not place your arms in front of your head. Place your stroke in front of your shoulders and move your body to get behind your arm with power.

The fingers, hand and arm set the tone for the body. A bent arm creates hip bend and "bent" swimming while a straight arm entry creates straighter swimming from finger to toe.

Your ten minute warm-up is all about breathing.

Your first ten minutes in the water is all about establishing breathing. Whether you are a novice or expert, understanding and controlling your breath, your oxygen and energy requirements is what the first ten minutes of your warm up is all about. You do it on the bike. You do it on the run. Plan on going easier the first ten minutes in the water to establish an exhale rhythm underwater as you swim.

Little known fact: Why is your first lap in the pool the fastest? Because your skin is dry and the water has not adhered to your skin as much as it will adhere to it later. Water adhering to water creates much more drag than air to water does.

Your thirty to forty minute swim is learning and applying techniques.

Approach swimming like you would "timed" golf. Imagine a PGA tournament being scored by strokes and time on course. You would need good technique and aerobic endurance. Did you know that they do have an event like that created by Steve Scott, former American mile record holder? Steve Scott scored a 92 on an 18-hole course in less than thirty minutes. Imagine, how many spouses would be happier with a thirty minute round of golf?

Technique is a wonderful thing, if you have it. Until you have it, you need to work on it. However, finding someone who can teach you the correct technique is key. There are too many people who will likely tell you the opposite of what you need to do, simply because they are following a land-based paradigm. There are even fewer people who have the eye and are natural teachers. Your progress depends on the instructors and your ability too. You can also come to me if you like my approach.

Positional and performance swim drills.

Positional drills teach you the positions you need to achieve while swimming. Learn positional drill techniques first. Unless you know where your hands, arms, head, legs and body need to be, your performance will suffer. Again, there is so much interpretation (misinformation) about position that your best choice is to go with a proven coach. The positional drills that you would learn from me are: moving your underwater exhale from mouth to nose; centering your weight at your chest rather than your hips; using your hand and arm to set the tone and lead the body; throwing before rowing; underwater swimming; and shoulder strokes so your stroke enters the water at your point of flexibility. You would learn to go against your land-based instincts and split the effort between the arms to reduce the workload.

Performance drill techniques teach you how to move through the positions with an awareness of your energy expenditure. In running, there are drills like bounding, high knees and skipping that can make you more aware of running motions. In swimming there are also performance drills. The performance drills that I teach give the feeling of bounding through the water, quickly striking the water, underwater drum beats, running fingers on the surface, and a shoulder shrug drill to effectively do the "crawl". You will learn that each performance drill has a different feel and different energy requirement. The benefit to the performance drills is that you can adjust your swim based on your changing conditions and energy level.

If you do come for lessons, be prepared to try new techniques quickly. Mistakes are allowed and encouraged. My favorite words are "Give it a try."

If you scrimp in paying for good coaching, you might have to spend the money over (and maybe over again) until you find a qualified instructor. Perhaps it makes sense to see if the local lifeguard can teach you how to swim. However, if you are not experiencing big changes in your comfort in the water and your ability to swim, consider hiring a professional swim coach and not just another swimmer to teach you how to swim.

Vary your strokes and stroke technique while swimming to vary the energy required.

When you first start swimming, you probably know only one speed. Maybe you go as fast as you can to "get it over with". Or, maybe you're a floater hoping the current will take you where you want to go. You will enjoy swimming more if you know all the "gears" in between sprinting and floating.

Your body and your brain will thank you when you learn various swim patterns and strokes. You can train yourself to use one muscle group more than another when you swim, much like you do in cycling when you get out of the saddle. You can take your swimming to a new level of performance and comfort by adding variety.

Your brain improves while swimming.

A real health benefit while swimming may come from what swimming does for your brain. In John J. Ratey, MD book, *Spark* Little, Brown and Company 2008, the author discusses how sports that require technique will develop the brain. Aerobic and technical sports improve the brain's executive function. The executive function helps you to rapidly recognize a situation and make decisions. It takes a while to develop the spark of how to swim correctly. Because you center your weight differently and exhale differently than you would on land, it takes you a while to learn the difference.

Your ten-minute cool down is all about recovery and breathing.

The ten-minute cool down swim that I am referring to now is after your bike and run. This is not an additional ten minutes to your 30 to 40 minute swim on your easy days.

Your swim after your bike and run is to begin the recovery process. Just walking in the water will help your body cool down. Did you know that the pressure of the water helps your veins move your blood back to your heart? The water pressure adds about a ten percent pumping effect back to the heart acting as an additional ventricle pump. So if you do nothing more than a ten-minute cool down walk in the pool, that's acceptable.

To go one better, work on breathing during your cool down. Remember the underwater exhale. Whether you are walking or swimming, "It's out with the bad air and in with the good air" to speed recovery. You can do this while walking in the pool or swimming.

To make the recovery swim even more worthwhile, notice your swimming pace after your bike and run. Like any race, it's easy to start a triathlon at a pace you can't keep up. If you can only swim "so fast" after the bike and the run, maybe your swim pace was too fast at the start of the triathlon.

You might also be kicking less while swimming after your bike and run. Kicking less is a long-term goal. Kicking is fine for sprinters, yet it has a terrible ROO (Return On Oxygen) for the distance swimmer over four hundred yards and the triathlete.

Passing people in the first transition, after your swim, is a good strategy and sign.

When you come out the water, in control and not out of breath, you can pass people. As far as the final result goes, ten seconds faster in the transition is equal to ten seconds faster in the water. And due to water resistance and drag, picking up ten seconds on land will be easier than picking up ten seconds in the water. Use that to your advantage.

When you look forward to your swim, the program's goal is accomplished.

Your technical ability to swim is crucial to outdoor swimming. If you don't have it, you won't be in control. You will wonder if you're even swimming in a straight line while outdoors. You will be praying while swimming (the fox hole and hospital beds aren't the only place for conversions) if you don't have your technique down.

You know you are getting it right when two things happen. First, you look forward to a cool down swim after a bike and run. Second, your placing in the swim moves closer to your placing in the bike and the run.

Practice getting low over the handle bars indoors, so you develop the strength and flexibility to do so outdoors. In this position, you can power over the pedals while staying low to reduce wind drag.

Relative to the other two events, this is where most time is spent.

You have to love the bike too. You will spend as much time on the bike as the other two events combined. Some triathletes achieve 5 to 10 minute leads on the bike, making it virtually impossible for the competition to catch them on the run.

If you want aerobic gains, weight loss and power, then it is best to accomplish these goals on the bike. Jack Foster, New Zealand, was a competitive cyclist first and then turned to running in his forties. Jack could run marathons in two hours and twelve minutes because he had a very positive carry over from cycling to running. Even while he was running marathons, Foster would do a 4 to 5 hour bike ride on Sunday instead of a long run.

The beauty of the bike is that it supports your weight. You can ride far longer than you can run because your body's weight is carried by the bike. The benefit of riding for longer periods is that it will force your body to develop the arterioles and capillaries in your legs by keeping the blood pressure up and working to adapt. The weight bearing support will also help prevent injury. An indoor bike is probably the safest way to train, so it's beneficial that this is where you spend most of your time training.

If you are new or it has been a while, the first class will be the hardest.

How hard can it be to sit on a bike? When I was teenager riding without padded cycling shorts, the seat rubbed me raw during a two-hour ride. *Ouch.* If I had also had firm cycling shoes, instead of flimsy tennis shoes, I could have put more pressure on my sore feet to take the pressure off my sore rear.

When you start cycling, you might find the seat and your feet hurt more than your legs. Obviously it helps to have cycling or triathlon shorts to protect your rear. It helps to have cycling shoes to support your feet. Make certain that both feel comfortable. Comfort and performance are very closely related when you are going to be sitting down for most of the triathlon.

Adjust your spin bike so it is comfortable.

Most spin class instructors and participants will help a new rider adjust the bike. The more adjustments available on the bike the better. Their help will get you about eighty percent of the way to your correct position on the bike. What no one in the spin class can take into account though is your (lack of) flexibility. There are standard formulas: if your leg is so tall, your seat or saddle needs to be so high. However, if you are not very flexible, the seat needs to be lowered so you do not strain your hamstrings. If you feel your hamstrings tightening, lowering your seat can help. However, too low a seat can hurt the knees. Once you are eighty percent there with the help of others, the final tweaking will be up to you.

Find four comfortable positions on your bike.

Unfortunately, pictures of the triathlon lead you to think that there is only one position on the bike in the triathlon. The picture of a triathlete as low as they can be on their triathlon bars and headed into the wind is the most common picture.

First, the most comfortable position is when the wind is at your back and you are sitting straight up. If the wind is behind you enough to where you can feel it pushing you, let the wind push you. Sit up straight like a sail and catch the wind. Your rear end will also thank you for the adjustment. Sitting straight up is also an alternative position when you're climbing a hill and there is no wind.

Second, leaning forward at a forty-five degree angle splits your weight between your upper body and seat. This position makes it very easy to steer or brake. When riding behind others outdoors, it is the safest and most comfortable position to be in while cycling. Let others break the wind while you draft, eat, drink and socialize. What's not to like about riding like this when you can?

Third, getting out of the saddle and riding is a real break for the rear end. For triathlon purposes, though, spin classes do too much power riding or uphill riding out of the saddle. On the road, you are never out of the saddle unless you are sprinting, climbing a steep hill, or you want to give your rear end an air freshening break.

Fourth position is being on your triathlon bars or the "drops" (the lowest part of your road bars). This is a comfortable position too, once your back and neck become more flexible and used to the position. Your weight is split between the arms and seat. You catch less wind outdoors. And you can get over the pedals better than when you are seated upright or at a forty-five degree angle.

Indoors, you will be more comfortable and more powerful spending some time in all four positions. Pretend that you are riding outdoors while training indoors. Imagine riding fast or into a strong head wind and you want to be low on your bars. Imagine a steep hill where you will want to get out of the saddle to power up the hill and give your rear end a break. Imagine a technical part of the course where you will need to make turns or get something to eat and want to be seated at the forty-five degree angle. Finally, imagine the wind at your back or on a long hill where you will be sitting up straighter. Having four comfortable positions to move in and out of will take that seat out of your rear end and make the bike a more comfortable and faster ride.

Outdoors, your mix will probably be eighty percent down low and twenty percent in the other three positions. This could be the opposite of what a spin class does, so adjust accordingly by doing what you need to do versus what they are doing. Not giving into spin class peer pressure goes right along with being a triathlete.

Drink and eat while riding indoors.

While riding indoors, refuel. Like outdoors, riding is your best opportunity to drink and eat.

Drinking and eating help you go faster and recover faster. You can compare training runs when you didn't have something to eat or drink with those when you did. Indoors is a great place to test which drinks and food work best for you. Then when you do race outdoors, don't change or add to your routine. Whatever you were drinking or eating 150-200 times a year in training will work just fine when racing.

Enjoy the music. It's your road.

I used to think that riding indoors was boring. OK. It is more boring than outdoors. Yet good music with some variety can help a great deal. The tempo of the music can be the tempo of your spin or cadence. If the beat is a steady ninety beats per minute, then spin with the beat at ninety beats per minute. If the beat slows to sixty beats per minute, get out of the saddle and push a bigger gear as if you are going uphill. If the music takes off, you can take off and sprint.

A good spin instructor will vary the music. Country music can be good for climbing. Techno music is good for spinning fast. Some rock 'n' roll is good for heads down, into the wind, low on the bike riding. A large part of the spin class value is that someone picked the music and will lead you through it. You can imagine each class as a new road that you have not been down yet. Enjoy the ride as you can go as hard or easy as you choose.

Music and tempo aids are illegal according to USAT regulations, so do learn your optimal tempo without music too. If you are choosing your own music, keep in mind that you will want a beat that is usually above ninety beats per minute.

If you have no music, you can also do this routine:

One minute seated upright spinning for recovery. One minute at the forty-five degree angle with a little more resistance. Two minutes in the low or down position, imagining that you are trying to stay low into the wind with even more resistance on the bike. One minute out of the saddle with more resistance on the bike like you are climbing a short hill. Five minutes done. Repeat.

In thirty minutes you will have six down hills, six flat roads, six sections into the wind and six short up hills. Not a bad training ride by yourself to imitate what is likely to happen outdoors.

Spin so your heart does more work than your legs.

It's easy to admire what Lance Armstrong and his long-time coach, Chris Carmichael, did in cycling. Early in his cycling career, Lance pushed a bigger gear and had success. After surviving cancer though, Carmichael changed Lance into a spinner. To paraphrase Carmichael, "When you push a bigger gear, your legs get tired. When you spin a smaller gear your heart gets tired. We know that the legs tire before the heart."

What is "spinning"? If your running cadence is ninety steps per minute, a spinning cadence would be anything above ninety. You are not spinning on the bike if your cadence is slower than your running cadence. You are pushing the pedals rather than spinning the pedals if your cycling leg speed is slower than running leg speed.

Some time trial specialists and triathletes adopt a big a gear approach as they can push with good results. However, some of the downsides are tired legs, knee injury and a loss of leg speed. The benefits of spinning is that you are "eating up the road" in small bites rather than big bites using your heart more than your legs to propel you.

Spin for recovery.

Most triathletes spend the last couple minutes on the bike spinning before they get off. Spinning at the end of the bike ride helps prepare your legs for the run and helps them recover.

Rik Van Looy was an impressive Belgium rider in the 1950s and '60s. He was the "King of the Classics" with many wins, like Paris-Roubaix, and World Championships to his credit. His secret: after a 5 to 6 hour race, HE WOULD GO INDOORS and ride on rollers to spin easily for an hour to help his legs recover.

Spend the last minute on the bike spinning easily before you get off. If you want to damage your run before you even take a step, just load your legs up on lactic acid by pushing a big gear to the end. However, if you want fresh(er) legs when you get off the bike, spin easily for at least a minute to allow the lactic acid to leave your legs. This will also make for a safer transition if you are not "screaming" into the transition at full speed on the bike.

Push for strength, like you wish you had an easier gear.

There are times when you have to push a bigger gear on the road, so add more resistance than you would like indoors to replicate the experience.

In real life, you will find hills that are steeper than you would like and head winds stronger than you would want. Prepare for them. No one escapes adversity. If you live in a flat part of the country, you deal with wind. If you live in a hilly or mountainous part of the country, you deal with climbs. Mimic what you will experience on the road indoors and push a big gear to prepare yourself.

Learn to get low and out of the wind indoors.

After getting used to the seat and the feet comes getting used to bending lower and lower for longer and longer periods of time. A flexible back helps. Your back can become more flexible over the duration of a class and more permanently flexible over time. A strong neck helps. Your neck can become stronger and more flexible likewise.

Ease into a lower position on the bike. Relax. Consider being low an option that you have so you don't get tired of any one position.

Look up, even when you are indoors. A bad habit that is easy to acquire indoors is allowing your head to droop. If you do this outdoors, you are likely to hit something if you are not looking up and forward. Practice looking forward indoors or you won't have the neck strength, flexibility and habit to do it outdoors.

As mentioned earlier, many spin classes do not spend much time in a low position on the indoor bike. To vary your training, you can get low on the bars when the class is on a moderate hill or sprinting. In a real life triathlon, you are not going to be sprinting. You will have steady accelerations, so change those indoor sprints into steady accelerations low on the bars. You could also turn your moderate uphills into low bar, "head wind" situations. In a triathlon, you seldom get out of the saddle unless there is a steep hill or no wind.

Here is a chart from Cycling Performance Tips to illustrate the point about wind resistance and speed. Notice how the caloric or energy requirement increases as your speed increases, making it important to ride low to minimize the effect of air resistance. The triathlon is all about saving calories and energy so you can excel or finish. Stay low or go slow.

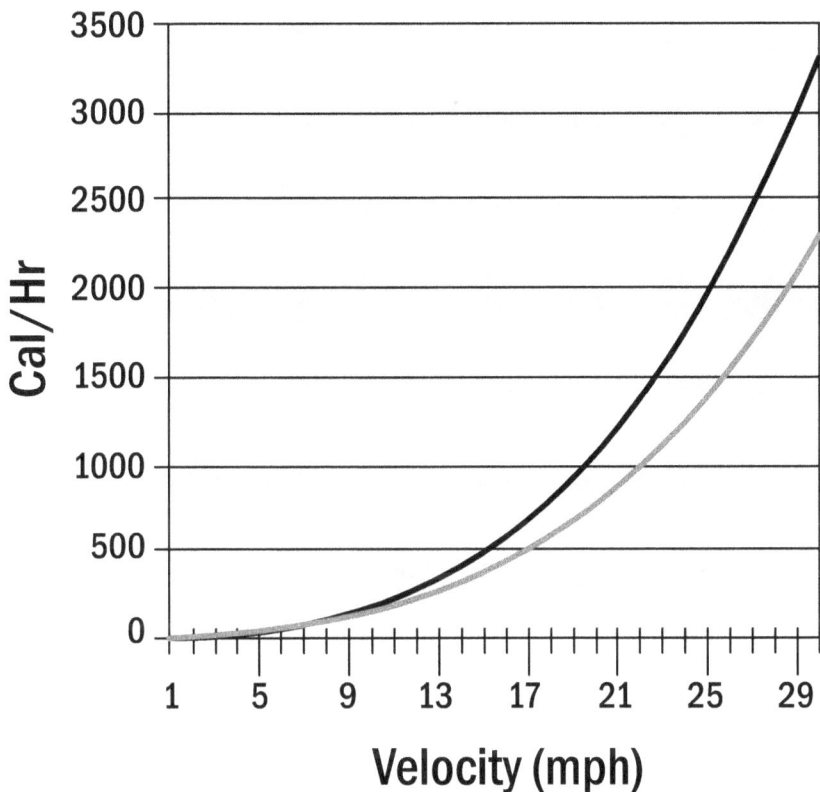

Learn to ride high to take advantage of the wind.

On the other hand, if you live in flat country, you know the experience of a twenty plus mile an hour wind literally blowing you home. A strong wind can be like riding up and downhill. Once you have the wind to your back, sail along by sitting more upright. Indoors, imagine yourself seated upright and spinning with the wind at your back. Here is your chance to eat, drink and be merry. Spin your legs to get the lactic acid out. Get out of the saddle to give your seat a break. Like downhills and uphills though, the time when the wind is at your back is shorter than the time when the wind is in your face.

In spin class or alone on the bike, be at your best.

Your bike ride takes up the most time. Your bike ride can aid your running. Your bike carries your weight, reduces your odds of injury and has "adjustable" positions. Work at being your best on the bike for the aforementioned reasons.

If you could pick one of the three events at which to excel, I would recommend the bike. It would be better to be highly placed on the bike, followed by the run and then swim rather than any other combination. You could be first out of the water and be passed before the race is over. You could catch a lot of people on the run, yet be so far behind after the bike that you never win. The bike ride is where you will achieve your best triathlon.

When you get off the bike hydrated, refueled and ready to run, goal accomplished.

Don't leave it "all" on the bike though. Just like your swim, you want to complete the bike ready for the next race within the race, the run.

If you drank enough while on the bike, you will be hydrated. If you ate on the bike, which is an especially good idea if you are doing an Olympic distance triathlon, you won't need to eat on the run. If you have something left in your legs after the bike, you will be looking forward to the run to the finish.

An especially important benefit of doing 150-200 indoor triathlons a year in training is that your body will adapt, and know how much you can push on the bike and still run effectively. You will probably go from walking to running after a few days or weeks. From there, your legs will get used to the transition faster and your ten-minute running pace could go to an eight-minute pace or faster after two years.

Your goal is to finish one part of the race looking forward to the next part. Emotionally, you want to be on the upswing during your triathlon. Train like it.

Comparing bike placement to swimming and running is useful information.

After you have raced, more important than your times are your placements in each race. If your placements were nice round numbers like 100th place on the bike, 1000th place on the swim and 500th place on the run, you know that you need to work on the swim. You have the bike down and the run will improve. You could go less hard on the bike and save your legs for the run. Or, you might need to hydrate and eat better on the bike so you don't run out of gas on the run.

Solving your triathlon puzzle for your best results is an interesting challenge that will be helped by doing it 150-200 times a year. Triathlons attract a pretty smart crowd who are trying to figure out how to do their best too. Use your placement, rather than time, in relationship to others to guide your training in order to improve.

Buy a road bike, not a triathlon bike at this stage. Or use your existing bike.

Have you ever heard of someone making the mistake of buying a special pair of running shoes for "the big race" and saving them for race day, only to blister their feet or find out the shoes did not fit?

The same can be true for your bike. Buying a triathlon bike to train and race with when you are first starting can be a big mistake. Did you know that triathlon bikes were not meant for steering and traffic? Triathlon bikes are made for roads without cars, fewer corners and a world without dogs and pedestrians.

You buy a road bike for the ability to steer and brake comfortably when you begin. If you want the world to know that you are training for a triathlon, like I do, you can buy clip on triathlon bars, the bars will only be somewhat in your way. For a sprint triathlon especially, your ability to steer your bike will be just as important as your ability to get low.

Like the beginning runner who would be wise to race in their training shoes, race on your training bike to reduce your odds of making mistakes on your ride.

Float running, as shown, develops stride length. The focus is to work on bringing your heel closer to your rear end while running as Bill is doing here.

Your weekly time trial measures your improvement.

Once a week, you will be running your own personal time trial on the treadmill. Your goal is to run .01 miles further per week after you get off your bike. Improve in the smallest measurable increments that the treadmill records. If you ran 2.02 miles in twenty minutes the week before, your goal would be to run 2.03 miles in twenty minutes the following week. Do this every week for a year and you will be running around 2.54 miles in twenty minutes. Do this for two years and you could be running over 3.00 miles in twenty minutes. Pretty fast running after a bike ride.

If you have the patience, you would do what Arthur Lydiard recommended beginners do in their first two years: focus on your training, no racing or very limited racing, improve steadily, and then plan your big race.

Arthur knew that aerobic gains come very slowly and over time. Racing and hard anaerobic work like intervals actually delay your aerobic gains because hard anaerobic work arrives at a diminishing chemical plateau and then declines, while aerobic gains do not. Your choice is keeping your training aerobic and improving, or doing intervals and racing to get official race results to your credit.

Your gains in each event, and in this program, will not come by racing. Your gains will come by training the same amount of time, yet going just a little further. Under Arthur's guidance I went from running seven miles an hour to ten miles an hour several years later. Pretty fast. It still feels good to remember this steady progression happened by following Arthur's program. It took me years to do this in the smallest increments that I could measure. Outdoors, I was happy to be just a few feet or yards further than the week before. Yet, I never had a year that was slower than the last until I became a recreational runner.

One of the beauties of this program is that your progression occurs with a certain momentum that is hard to stop when you train almost day in and day out. Your capillaries will be developing to deliver more oxygen to your muscles. The concept that your lungs and heart change is not quite as true as changes are occurring at the cellular level. Your body will change at the level of chemical and electrical interaction physiologically. Aerobic growth at the cellular level is not measurable in the short term by minutes. It is only measurable in the smallest noticeable increments, seconds or feet over a period of twenty minutes.

Aerobic improvement is endless according to Arthur Lydiard. Anaerobic improvement is not endless and decreases as we age. If you stick with this aerobic program, expect endless improvement in the smallest increments that you can measure.

Learn your pace from your weekly time trial.

Time trials were designed to help you learn your pace. A common mistake you can make is beginning your run too fast. Many of us have too much hare and not enough tortoise in us. Are you the type that starts out too fast? Your weekly time trial will help you develop your pace and your inner clock.

The hare in you wants to run as fast as you can NOW. If you are feeling good after the bike, you might feel like you could run not just a hundredth of a mile (.01) further today, but a tenth of a mile (.1) further. A weekly improvement of a hundredth of a mile, seventeen yards, over twenty minutes is doable. A weekly improvement of a tenth of a mile, one hundred and seventy-six yards, is not sustainable.

It's tempting to think that you can occasionally improve by leaps and bounds. Don't be fooled though. The treadmill will teach you that if you start out too fast, you will have a hard time holding on to your pace for twenty minutes. You could possibly run even slower than the previous week.

Even if you do make a time trial gain of faster than .01 or seventeen yards, you are likely to plateau or regress later. If you make a gain from 2.12 to 2.14 in one week, accept a 2.13 or a 2.14 time trial the following week. You will end up racing your time trials if you go for more gains than your body can physiologically deliver. And racing your training is its own personal hell.

Developing the clock within you is a confidence builder. You will know your pace so well that you can go beyond the level of recognizing the difference between an eight-minute mile and a ten-minute mile. You could get the feeling down to knowing your pace, plus or minus five seconds per mile. This is helpful information for training and racing.

The Indoor Triathlete program focuses on feedback and information from your training for your improvement. Following the program will teach you about yourself, successfully. Your performance gains come as your body slowly learns, through repetition, what it is completely capable of doing. Running a twenty-minute time trial weekly, fifty time trials in a year, will give you the confidence to race a triathlon, at your pace, any day of the year.

Relative to the other two, you can always walk.

Whether you are competing in your first triathlon or your tenth, you can always walk in order to finish or win. Walk and eventually win a race? Yes, and it's happened more than once. Good places to walk in a triathlon include: uphill, out of sight, around drink stations, and anywhere you feel like it to avoid injury in order to finish.

Jeff Galloway did the running world a tremendous service by re-introducing the concept of walking in order to finish a marathon. You don't have to pass out and die, like Phidippides did, at the end of your race. It is ironic though that Galloway named his running stores after Phidippides, a person who did die, yet Galloway coaches runners to walk in order to finish their marathons.

Race directors, volunteers and your family won't like it if you refuse to walk and you pass out. Your other competitors may take your passing out as a sign of the tough triathlon that they completed. So if you want to be an ego boost for your competition, just run until you pass out or crawl across the finish line.

There is no shame in walking. And walking can be done strategically.

Get used to walking or running after biking.

On your first attempts when you are walking or running after the bike it's going to feel awkward. This may last for days, weeks or months. After your body gets the message that you are serious and are going to continue to run after your bike, your body starts shaping up. You may actually get to the point where you might be running faster off the bike compared to starting a run without a warm-up.

During a real triathlon, you won't want to spend more time than you need to spend in the transition between bike and run. Time you spend in the transitions would probably be better spent moving down the road. Indoors though you realistically cannot go from the bike to the treadmill in seconds. Common courtesy means that you will probably wipe your spin bike off before going to the treadmill. Or, you might expect someone to say something to you about hygiene if you don't. It's also not a common practice to run indoors from bike to treadmill. Plan on wiping down the bike and walking to the treadmill for at least a two-minute transition.

Have your running shoes at your bike to speed up the transition. Wipe off your bike one minute before class is over so you are not waiting in line for paper towels and spray. Walk directly to the treadmill in your bike shoes. Sit on the treadmill and change into your running shoes and begin.

The treadmills often have a Quick Start button. Hit that button. Add a .5 incline. Speed up the treadmill as fast as you can handle or as slow as you need to go. As you adapt during the run, bump up the speed by .1 miles per hour when you feel ready. Most treadmills have timers so you know when your ten or twenty minutes is over for this program. Half way through your time, you can take off the .5 incline and go at a 0.0 incline. The treadmills will also measure distance covered, calories and more. If you start doing the numbers in your head, you might also find that you can also get good at basic math, which will come in handy while racing.

After EVERY training run (I think this is the only absolute that I use in this book), you need to feel like you could have run faster. Whether it's your weekly time trial or your long run, do not train as if you could not have run any faster that day. If you did, you were not training. You were racing. You were inviting injury and illness into your indoor triathlete program. Don't run at full capacity unless there is a banner down the road that reads FINISH LINE. And even then, if you do, you might screw up tomorrow's training, which is against your first rule. Don't do anything today that will screw up tomorrow.

"Float running" is to improve your running technique.

You are more likely to feel your age while running compared to swimming or cycling. After much research and observation, the number one culprit for our slow down (drum roll please) is that *older runners don't bring their heels as close to their rear as they used to when running.*

The researchers are right. Arthur Lydiard had us doing drills to increase our awareness and ability to bring the leg closer and closer to our rear ends when running. Start making this one change to your running and walking at this time. Focus on bringing your heel higher and closer to your rear end as you walk and run.

When you first try bringing your heel closer to your rear, you can expect to feel your quadriceps squeeze—it's probably been a while since you have done this maneuver. You may actually feel less coordination until your legs and body re-learn the movement. You might have some steps that feel like you are clopping along. It will be OK. Over time, you can learn to run like a child again if you become more aware of this child-like running movement.

Twice a week in the program you will be doing a "float" run. Your only emphasis is to get those heels up traveling closer and closer to your rear end. Ten minutes is enough. Your legs will already be warmed up from the bike ride so just lift the legs up behind you. When you feel more airborne, both feet off the ground, you are on the right track. Some strides will eventually feel like you are floating for a moment between each foot strike.

Float running, by bringing your heel up closer to your rear, works. The reason that the float works is that it increases your stride length. It is easier and takes less energy, to increase your stride length by keeping the leg airborne a little longer rather than pushing off the ground a little harder.

There are many running techniques that Arthur taught which are still proving valid. This is the most valuable one that you will need at this time. Once you get used to this movement, it could be worthwhile to do more running drills, yet let's not change too much too fast and invite injury.

A long run at race distance.

In your program, there will be one long run, thirty minutes to an hour, after a bike. Thirty minutes to an hour will take care of the time needed for a sprint or Olympic distance triathlon. If you can cover a mile every ten minutes, this will do it.

Take it easy on the long run. Your goal is to put in the time and get used to the road. When conditions permit, do this run outdoors.

Like the time trial, over time you will be able to cover more and more distance. While you will be aware of your improvement, it would be better if you don't measure this run or run the same course week after week.

Like an outdoor swim or bike, you will get more from your long outdoor run if you notice the scenery and how you are feeling. Once you have that information, you will have had a good bike then long run and you are ready for a ten-minute cool down in the water.

The transformation that you want from weightlifting and stretching as an indoor triathlete.

Your muscles are like a series of chains linked together. The central or core chain links are in the center of your body, your abdominal muscles and back muscles. If your central chain links tire, give or break, the outer chain links are much less effective and could be useless. At the beginning of your program, you might have to temporarily lift less weight with your arms and legs if you are already strong in those areas, and build your core chain links to match the chain links in your arms and legs.

You want to change from having strong legs or strong arms to having a strong body. Your muscles have weight that you have to carry and support. While muscle looks great, do you really want to race for hours carrying those "guns" that you will never fire? It's not like you can punch your competition in a triathlon. If you bulk up your biceps beyond your core strength, then the core tires and strains.

Think of yourself as being able to lift fifty pounds with every part of your body, or seventy-five pounds with every part of your body, or a hundred pounds with every part of your body. Do not lift or manage fifty pounds of weight with your core and then a hundred and fifty pounds with your arms unless you want to strain your core. Your fifty pound core doesn't necessarily want to carry arms that can lift a hundred and fifty pounds throughout a triathlon either.

Balanced strength prevents injuries.

Your weightlifting is also in conjunction with your stretching. Your movement while lifting is to stretch while extending and contracting. Lifting in this manner gives you important information about your flexibility and strength while using the muscle. You want to feel a stretch, and if there is any soreness while lifting you need to know that information on your recovery day of weightlifting. If you feel a pain, use the pain to guide your training. Use little pains to determine if a technical change to your swim, bike or run is needed; or rest is needed; or more balanced strengthening is needed, before little pains become big pains.

Injuries can occur when there is an imbalance in muscle strength. For example, if you have strained hamstrings, it could be that you can only lift ten or twenty pounds with your hamstrings while you could be lifting a hundred pounds with your quadriceps. If your quadriceps are stronger than your hamstrings, your hamstrings may succumb to injury. To overcome your strained hamstrings, you need to temporarily reduce the amount that you are lifting with your quadriceps while increasing the amount your hamstrings are lifting until you are lifting the same weight with both your quadriceps and hamstrings. Just stretching the hamstrings without resistance or just resting the hamstrings by sitting on them could make the situation worse. Sometimes you can proactively heal with weightlifting.

Your weightlifting days are your recovery days. You are making a big mistake if you feel tired the day after weightlifting because you were doing more than just balancing your muscle groups and your chain links. *Swim, bike, run, recover* is the indoor triathlete's motto, and the day that you have for recovery is the day you should lift weight for feedback and information.

Your goals with your weight training are muscle balance, flexibility, feedback and recovery. You want to know your weak spots. You want to eliminate weak spots in your chain, starting with your core. You want your weight training to be a recovery workout. When you are done with the weights, the information that you want is: did something hurt, and how was my range of motion? Knowing if you have a muscle imbalance and acting upon that information is more important than lifting more weight.

Determine your core strength.

Use weight machines that will let you know how much you can lift with your upper core and your lower core. As I define it, your upper core is above your belly button. Your lower core is below your belly button. If you are like most people, your upper core will be stronger than your lower core because of everyday land-based activity. You will want to be as strong below the belly button as you are above the belly button to reduce lower back stress, and prevent herniation and soreness. Strength below the belly button will also work wonders for your swim.

A lack of lower core strength shows up in your swimming when your hips give and drop when you are on your back or rolling for air. The lack of lower core strength creates a break in the chain strength that you want to have while swimming.

Extend your core strength to your arms and legs.

Improving your core strength and then extending it to your arms and legs is the safe way to train. If your core strength can lift fifty pounds and you are lifting a hundred pounds with your arms or legs you could strain your torso and end up with a sore back. If you can only lift fifty pounds with your upper and lower abdominal core muscles, it won't do you much good if you are lifting double and triple that weight with your arms and legs.

Don't even try to see how much you can lift.

Under the category of don't do anything today that will screw up tomorrow, don't try to see how much you can lift. You are not in a weightlifting competition. It would be a mistake to see how much you can lift. Seeing how much you can lift is an exercise in vanity and is to be avoided. If you are having trouble lifting a weight six times, you are trying to lift too much weight. You would be better off reducing the weight until your strength increases in a balanced way.

Keep your weightlifting aerobic and varied.

If your club has twenty to forty machines for weightlifting, try them all. It's not uncommon to workout on twenty different machines in thirty minutes. You do six to twelve repetitions on one machine for your back. Then you go to another weightlifting machine for your muscles in your back and do another six to twelve repetitions. You might even want to go to a third or fourth machine to work on building up your back before moving on to build up your chest, arms and legs.

Be patient with weightlifting.

Your program is a progression of the smallest measurable increments. Although weights are usually in five-pound increments, if you move up from ten to eleven repetitions that's progress.

Measure progress by your body's responses and core strength gains.

The better you become at analyzing your body's strengths and weaknesses, the more effective weight training will be for you. Day to day life can make your muscles sore. Your weight training program is NOT supposed to make them even more sore. Weight training is designed to help sore muscles repair by doing a stretch and strengthen movement.

Measure your gains by doing more sit-ups and lower abdominal crunches, with or without weights. After that feedback, at the beginning of your weightlifting session, you can move on to doing more or less weights with your back, arms and legs.

Be prepared to lift LESS weight on some days.

While you might like to think of weightlifting as a steady progression, be happy that weights are helping you to analyze where you are on any given day. Be satisfied that weights are your easy, recovery workout that sets up success for your aerobic days. Use weights to strengthen and stretch your muscles through a range of motions. Know that feedback from lifting weights means that you will be lifting less weight on some days because of how you feel due to injury or fatigue.

Five minutes off the floor to test your functional core strength.

Finally, to get feedback on how functional your core strength is, lie down and keep your feet and legs off the ground for five minutes. You can move your feet up and around, kick or hold them still. You can roll from your back to face down and then back again. You'll want to know how your core is supporting your legs and arms. Keeping your legs off the floor gives you good feedback as to the extent of your lower core strength. If your lower core is strong, it will be possible to keep your legs off the floor for five minutes. Every other weightlifting day or session, do five minutes off the floor rather than weightlifting with your abdominal muscles for this feedback.

Value feedback more than performance.

Like weightlifting, stretching with resistance provides you with helpful information. The information that your body gives you is important to your health. Pay attention. Knowing that something does or does not hurt is valuable information. You use that information to guide your training.

It never impresses me afterward if I hurt myself stretching as I occasionally do in yoga trying to keep up with others.

Stretching with the ability to resist the stretch, not going to your farthest lengths, is like low-level weightlifting. Stretching in this way provides you with subtle feedback on how hard your last workout was on your body so you know if you need to take it easier next time in order to make progress.

Best time to stretch for feedback.

The best time to stretch for feedback, in the Indoor Triathlete program, is before you go to bed on your bike, run, swim days. By the time you are ready to go to bed, your body has had some time to recover and feel either good or bad. Before sleeping, you will be able to stretch, with time less a factor, in order to properly assess how you are feeling.

If you stretch too soon after working out, you will still have adrenaline and endorphins in your body. Your body might say "It's all OK", when it's not. Or worse yet, if you are stretching and your body says "It's not OK" you could be further injuring yourself. Cool down your body with a recovery swim. Don't stretch to cool down.

Maybe the worst time to stretch is right before your workout for your "warm up". You are probably in a let's-get-going mood at this time. If your body said "Stop", would you stop at that time and modify your workout? Most people would find it hard to be dressed and ready to bike or swim and then not bike or swim because they just noticed an injury. Warm up your body by going slowly for the first ten minutes of the swim, bike or run. Don't stretch to warm up.

Don't even try to see how far you can stretch. Always be able to resist.

It's a mistake to check your progress by how far you can go while stretching. If you touched your toes two days ago, yet can't touch them today, you don't have a problem in and of itself. Forcing the stretch to touch the toes is likely to cause injury rather than feedback.

The benefit of resistance in stretching is that it keeps you from going too far with a stretch. Too often I go to a yoga class and try to extend beyond the point of contraction. Injury or muscle soreness then occurs. If you contract the muscle while extending the muscle, you are stretching properly.

The best book that I have found on stretching is *The Genius of Flexibility (Bob Cooley, Simon & Schuster, 2005)*. Dara Torres, the US Olympic Medalist swimmer, does similar resistance stretching called 'Chi Hara'.

You won't be able to do what a Pilates or yoga instructor does.

Unless you are very well practiced in yoga or Pilates, don't expect to strike the poses that your instructor can. If you go to these classes, go to get information. Some questions for the instructor are: "How do I modify this pose for me?" or "What is the benefit of the pose?" Certain stretches can help the kidneys, liver or thyroid for example.

Stretching and weightlifting makes you stronger than just weightlifting on its own.

Research is proving that a combination of stretching and weightlifting does more than just weightlifting alone. Michael R. Bracko, in the ACSM's Health and Fitness Journal, reports that the group also doing static stretching increased their one repetition maximum by 16%, 27% and 31% compared to those who only did weightlifting, who had gains of 12%, 14% and 9% in three lifting activities.

The best time to do static stretching is on the days you are not lifting weights, according to the report. In the Indoor Triathlete program, the time to stretch would be on your aerobic days. In fifteen to twenty minutes before going to bed, your stretching will help you recover from the swim, bike and run and set you up for greater gains. By the time you are ready to go to bed, some of the muscle soreness or tiredness will have settled in and you have more time to better analyze how you feel followed by rest.

The bag.

You need a bag that is always packed and ready to go. You could use an old laptop bag as it is flexible with plenty of pockets. The bag needs the capacity to hold your swim, bike and running gear. It also needs compartments to organize your accessories. If you pack for race day, every day, you will never want for anything while training or racing.

You will be surprised that you won't need an overly large bag. Swim suits, triathlon clothing and running clothing can be squished down rather easily. You do need the bag to fit in your cycling shoes and running shoes. Sandals are nice yet optional gear indoors. If the bag can take care of your shoes, your other gear and clothing can probably fit in around your shoes.

Pack what you need in one bag and keep your bag with you wherever you go. Bring your bag whenever you're in doubt about when you might do your workout. No bag. No workout. No race. Keep your triathlon bag packed, ready and with you at all times.

Goggles and suit.

Forgetting your goggles and swim suit tends to be a show-stopper. Pack an old or extra pair of goggles and suit in your bag, just in case you forget or your strap breaks. Use your extra pair once a month to be certain that they work for you just in case. You could swim without a swimsuit, in your gym shorts, yet you probably won't swim without your goggles.

Do pack your swim suit. Don't swim in your triathlon shorts. Swimming in chlorinated water in your triathlon shorts will soon wear them out. Triathlon shorts will be fine in the open water; however, chlorine loosens up triathlon shorts and you are left with baggy pants. Have a swim suit to change into after you run for your cool down swim.

Cycling shoes, shorts and shirt.

Cycling shoes are clunky everywhere other than on the bike. Get a pair of outdoor cycling shoes that you can use on your bike. While the rest of the spin class will probably have spin class cycling shoes, I don't really see the benefit of training in a spin shoe and then racing in a different shoe. Remember, your goal is to train like you race and vice versa. Having different training shoes from racing shoes could lead to problems down the road. Pun intended.

Your cycling shoes will probably need SPD® (Shimano Pedaling Dynamics) cleats. SPD cleats tend to be unique to spin classes and mountain bikes. You can also use SPD cleats on your road bike for outdoor triathlon training and racing. There are other good cleats for cycling but most indoor bikes already have SPD cleats.

Your cycling shoes need to be comfortably wide in the toe box and forefoot. Some cycling shoes are built on a narrow last for a narrow foot. Narrow cycling shoes that squeeze your forefoot can produce neuromas in the forefoot, cut off circulation and numb the feet. You can't go by cost when buying your shoes. A shoe fifty dollars cheaper maybe the right shoe for you. Going for pretty and matching colors is also a little shortsighted. If you want a matching outfit, buy the shoes first.

Your cycling shorts are a personal priority. Speedo brief swim suits can be used to function as cycling and running shorts too. Early in triathlon history, many triathletes just wore their swim briefs rather than jammers for the entire race. They would swim in them, ride in them and run in them. You can still do that outdoors. I would not advise it though or you will become an outcast. If you have to give it a try though, let every one know that you forgot your triathlon shorts, keep moving and don't be a show off. Indoors you probably don't want to wear a Speedo while riding in spin class or running on the treadmill.

For cycling shorts, you can go with swimming "jammers" or triathlon shorts. They both look similar. The jammers do not have a pad between you and saddle, while the triathlon shorts do. For the sake of some padding, most people use triathlon shorts. Of course, you could also use cycling shorts. Thick cycling short pads feel a little diaperish when running though.

For your triathlon shirt or jersey, you can go with or without pockets. Pockets are for food, keys and money. For a sprint triathlon, you probably won't need pockets for food. For a longer, Olympic distance triathlon, you will need pockets for food.

You don't want a baggy shirt that acts like a parachute. Buy or use a shirt that is form-fitting. You want a shirt or jersey that retains some sweat to keep you cool yet does not make you cold. Cotton is not good. Wool, silk or specially designed synthetic wear works well. If you want Under Armour® fine. If you want WalMart's Starter® brand for a much lower price, then go to Walmart®. I use Starter brand and it's worked well for several years.

Towels and extras.

An extra towel is about the most used extra that you will ever carry. If the extra towel is there, you are likely to use it. Have you considered hand towels? An extra hand towel can dry off the entire body and take less room to store and wash.

Eyeglasses. If you are like me, have an extra pair of glasses in your bag. I keep my sport glasses in my bag and my regular glasses on hand. Once I misplaced my glasses or they were taken by someone else, and I was glad that I had an extra pair for the drive home.

Extra socks. Change of clothes. Extra goggles. However, it can get to the point of having too much extra on hand. Like your closet at home, clean out your bag twice a year.

Where to put your race number.

Do not pin your race number on your clothing. You can buy, sometimes on race day, a triathlon race number belt for your number. After the swim, you put the belt with your number on it around your waist. The number goes in back while on the bike and in the front while running.

They will also body mark you with your number, gender and age. This is also handy information so you can see who you are passing or being passed by during a race.

Eat what you normally eat when beginning.

Too much and too little is made out of what you eat for optimal training and racing. When beginning, don't change your diet straightaway. Wait for your body to give you some training feedback and then start changing your diet.

Too often, the triathlon culture suggests that you live off their food: sports drinks, power bars and tofu. While you eventually might find those foods helpful, initially they could be a distraction. If you are starting or changing your training and changing your diet at the same time, how well could you identify what is right or wrong? How much of which change could you attribute to your training versus your diet? Settle into your training and let your body tell you what it wants during and after training.

Olympic runners used to drink de-fizzed colas. A bagel is like a sports bar. In your everyday diet, there are already foods that work.

It's OK to be calorie aware if you want to lose weight. I've known people who have had success with Weight Watchers® and other calorie counting programs. I don't buy into limiting or overloading on carbohydrates, fats or proteins. I do like natural foods. Food that I have seen growing naturally outdoors seem more trustworthy.

Begin with where you are. Don't change your breakfast from training day to race day. Don't change lunch or dinner. Wait until your body says it's time to cut back, or something else sounds good.

Practice drinking and eating on the bike.

Probably one of the biggest mistakes I made while marathon training was not drinking more while training. I imagined myself toughening up during the run and thought that any drink during a race would be a bonus. My training and racing suffered. I was dehydrated in training and I was spilling my drinks while racing. If I had practiced drinking on the run, I would have felt better and performed better.

When you are tired and moving, it's not easy to drink or eat. Having the coordination to ride with one hand while drinking with the other hand while out of breath and looking down the road takes practice.

With eating, you are breathing while you're chewing. You should practice on the bike in spin class or going down the road at a good speed. On the bike, you might find power bars handier than a bagel.

Practice sipping and pouring on the run.

It takes coordination to exhale before drinking. If you have been focusing on your exhale, as I advised, this will help your drinking. Exhale, drink, inhale.

When to eat on the bike.

On the bike, you want to eat. In a sprint triathlon, eating is optional. You may want to eat in the first ten or twenty minutes of the bike during a sprint triathlon for practice. In a sprint triathlon, because it's over so fast (fast being under two hours), the benefit of the fuel could be offset by digestive energy used.

In an Olympic distance triathlon, eating is not optional even if you can get the race done in close to two hours. Because your race is going to take two and a half to four hours, practice eating on the bike.

Because it takes a while to digest food, don't eat right before you get off the bike unless you have practiced it and have had good results.

When your body burns carbohydrates, fats and proteins.

Many people don't realize that the body does not burn fat until after forty minutes of exercise. During the first forty minutes, you are burning up the blood sugars and carbohydrates present when you started.

If you want to burn the fat on your body while training, your training must take you past forty minutes. And the longer you go past forty minutes, the more fat your body will burn. Burning more fat is one advantage of this program. Every workout has you going for an hour to two hours. In every workout, your body will burn fat. More impressively, your body will train itself to go from carbohydrate burning to fat burning more easily.

On the other hand, you do want to drink and eat while training and racing for two or more hours or your body will also start to burn up proteins (muscle). While marathon runners are naturally thin, training for over two hours a day without eating on the run keeps their muscle mass low.

If you are like me, you probably skipped to this section without reading the reasoning behind the program. That's OK, but do go back and forward to read the entire book.

Arthur Lydiard often said that "training schedules are not worth the paper they are written on." If your triathlon coach is telling you how many intervals in how many seconds to do, be very skeptical. The same goes for heart monitors. Intervals in seconds and heart rate is helpful information, yet it's better to base your training on your experience. You are likely to do those intervals too hard or too easy and the heart rate training will limit your growth.

Your training program will be based on time. Time is a very handy measurement. Scheduling your time is easier than scheduling your distance. When a half hour is up, it's up. Whereas if I said three miles, that could take anywhere from fifteen to thirty minutes depending on the person. Time allows the fit runner to cover ten miles in an hour while the beginner covers five miles in an hour. Arthur trained world champions and beginners by time and never distance. He trained champions and beginners based on how they felt, not what the schedule said that day or intervals per second.

The most remarked benefit of having a coach.

Training for years with many knowledgeable coaches and athletes has been a real education. The number one remark that top athletes make is that a good coach would have helped them FROM OVERTRAINING, ESPECIALLY BEFORE A BIG RACE.

You won't need my help in pushing yourself. I know people who want to train are pushing themselves. Most people do like a coach or someone to help hold them accountable for working out. Most people do like a knowledgeable coach who can tell them what to do next. Yet, the real value and art of coaching is demonstrated in the ability to hold back a good athlete and not overdo their training.

The first ten minutes, and it's never stretching.

When you start biking, running or swimming, start slow for the first ten minutes. Your sure sign that your body is ready for work is a sweat. No sweat, no go hard.

I think that stretching before a workout began when coaches wanted to stand around and pontificate about the workout. Maybe it was an organizational tool to keep athletes busy while listening. However, stretching a muscle that is not "sweating" invites injury.

Most spin class instructors know this, so I am less worried about this happening to you on the bike. While running or swimming though, work on establishing your breathing and wait for the sweat to happen before going harder

The hard days are biking, running and cool down in the pool.

Put your effort into those days where you are going to bike, run and swim. Put the most effort into your bike ride. Put good effort into your run, yet run like you saved something back and don't run all out. Swim like you are tired (you will be) and begin recovering during your swim.

You may feel great after the hard workout of bike, run and swim. Wait a few hours or a day though to determine how hard your workout was. You may not be able to tell if you are over training during and right after the workout due to the adrenaline and endorphins in your body.

If you want feedback and more recovery, do resistance or power stretching later in the day. When you feel sore or stiff, stretch for feedback and information. Don't overly stretch and make the situation worse. Like running, always hold something back while stretching, don't completely extend yourself. There is no FINISH sign in sight while you are stretching.

Don't do anything on a hard day that will screw up your easy day, tomorrow.

The easy days are pool and then weights.

Take it easy the next day in the pool. The first ten minutes in the pool is just to get used to the water temperature, exhaling often, and orienting your weight at your chest and not your hips. The next ten minutes is spent doing drills to work on your technique. The final ten to twenty minutes is swimming like you want to swim in a race. Sight in the pool often, like you will have to do outdoors.

Take it easy with the weights. Start with what your core can lift to determine what you can do. If you can lift forty pounds on one of the core machines with your abdominal muscles, do forty pounds around the gym. You are building your strength from the inside out. You probably have your outer strength ahead of your core strength. Give your core some time to catch up and give everything else a break. Remember tomorrow is a hard bike. All you want from weightlifting is feedback, balance in body strength and recovery.

Don't do anything on an easy day that will screw up your hard day tomorrow.

If needed, take a day off with no make ups or schedule adjustments.

In effect, your "hard" workouts are the bike and the run. Easy workouts or recovery workouts begin with the cool down swim after your run and the next day's swim and weightlifting.

If you need to take time off, take a day off.

Another mistake I made while cycling and marathon training was thinking that I needed to make up for missed training. It's not practical to do three hours the day after you missed a day of training. The benefit of not making up the training is more recovery. The risk of making up training is injury.

If you miss a Monday, do your Tuesday workout on Tuesday. If you miss Monday, Tuesday, Wednesday, Thursday and Friday, just do your Saturday workout on Saturday based on how you feel.

Your scheduled workouts, 365 days a year. Keep it simple.

Monday - Hard. 40 minute bike, 10 minute floating run, 10 minute recovery swim.

Tuesday - Easy. 30 minute swim and 30 minutes of weightlifting.

Wednesday - Hard. 30 minute bike, 20 minute running time trial, 10 minute recovery swim.

Thursday - Easy. 30 minute swim and 30 minutes of weightlifting.

Friday - Easy. 40 minute bike, 10 minute floating run, 10 minute recovery swim.

Saturday - Hard. 20 minute swim, 60 minute bike, 30 minute run, 10 minute recovery swim. If you can, do the bike and run outdoors where traffic is at a minimum. You want to experience handling your bike and running on something other than a treadmill.

Sunday - Easy. 30 minute swim and 30 minutes of weightlifting.

You can take any of the days off if you are too tired to train or if business or family demands require that you miss a day. When you miss a day, don't go back. Don't make it up. There is no sacred day of training.

On Friday, take it easy so you know what taking it easy on the bike, run and swim means. That information will come in handy later.

After three months or ninety days of this programmed training, if you want to add five or ten minutes here or there and train longer, go ahead. Until you have trained for three months, your body has probably not adjusted to the gradual workload increase, so don't increase the times below.

CALENDAR

MON	TUE	WED	THUR	FRI	SAT	SUN
Hard. 40 minute bike, 10 minute floating run, 10 minute recovery swim.	Easy. 30 minute swim 30 minutes of weightlifting.	Hard. 30 minute bike 20 minute running time trial 10 minute recovery swim.	Easy. 30 minute swim, 30 minutes of weightlifting.	Easy. 40 minute bike, 10 minute floating run, 10 minute recovery swim.	Hard. 20 minute swim, 60 minute bike, 30 minute run, 10 minute recovery swim.	Easy. 30 minute swim 30 minutes of weightlifting. Or, take a day off.

Swim where you will be seen.

More important than swimming with someone is being seen while swimming. You want to be seen by boats and someone on shore. Someone on shore can call for help faster than someone who has to swim to shore first.

Swimming with a poor swimmer is actually not a good idea. Unless you have had training as a lifeguard and know defensive rescue tactics, they could drown you. Do you mind swimming with someone who makes you wonder, "Are they going to make it?" Get used to the idea. There will be some poor swimmers in your triathlons.

Let people know where you will be swimming and ask them to keep an eye out for you if you are at a public beach. If you can arrange for a boat escort, do so, especially if you are swimming outside designated swimming areas.

Look, listen and ride like a car, out of traffic.

Do not ride facing cars. It's scary and against the law. Ride with your back to the cars and listen for their approach. Don't block out road noise by listening to music. Listening to music or any tempo setting device is also illegal in a triathlon. Ride with the traffic flow, listening for traffic as you go.

Look ahead for cars pulling out or turning in front of you. If they do not make eye contact with you, you cannot know if they have seen you.

In any collision, both you and your bike lose. Avoid collisions at all costs and don't risk running stop lights or signs.

YIELD. Yield says it all. The warning doesn't have to say cars, dogs, pedestrian, geese, wet roads, gravel, or other riders. When riding outdoors, yield, and put your adrenaline and ego aside.

The best traffic is no traffic. Find a time or a place to ride with minimal traffic.

Don't train so hard when outdoors that you find it hard to look ahead or handle your bike. A tired rider is a dangerous rider. You are more likely to stop looking ahead and look down, potentially hitting a pothole or hitting something or someone else. You will also find it harder to ride a straight line. Like Clair Young said, "It's the rider that is out of shape that is hard on their equipment. They are more likely to crash when tired and damage their bike."

Listen and run like a pedestrian, out of traffic.

When running, you *do* want to face traffic. You can easily jump up on the curb out of the way if needed while running. Most people probably can't do that on a bike. So running is the opposite of biking in this way. Run facing the traffic and listen to the traffic.

Do make eye contact with cars pulling out in front of you. If you don't make eye contact, don't act like you have the right of way. Be prepared to stop for cars. Yield.

The best traffic is no traffic. Find a time or a place to run with minimal traffic.

Practice your race while training.

In your head, in your thoughts, practice your race by thinking of race scenarios.

When you're swimming, think of what it will be like to swim with limited visibility and hundreds of people swimming to the same place where you want to swim.

When you are riding, train on the down bars, over the brakes, sitting upright and out of the saddle. Out of the saddle is going to feel completely different on a bike outdoors. The bike really squirms underneath you when you first get out of the saddle. Take it easy getting out of the saddle outdoors if you are not used to it. You will soon learn to limit your out of saddle riding to steep hills and airing out your sore rear end.

When you are running outdoors, get used to the feel of uphills and downhills. The treadmill can't replicate a downhill. You can learn to run down hills fast and you will enjoy the benefit and break of a gradual downhill.

The Indoor Triathlete has built in safeguards.

A real benefit of this program is that you seldom repeat activities day to day. If you felt sore from your bike or weightlifting you won't have a bike or weightlifting session the very next day to make the situation worse. You have a day to notice that you overdid it. And the program gives you that day away from the activity in order to rest and recover. You will more often notice an injury the day after you injure yourself.

Another benefit is that relatively easy weightlifting is a form of checks and balances on your triathlon activities. During weightlifting and stretching, your body will give you feedback when you are injured. When you discover an injury with weightlifting and stretching, use that information to work the antagonistic muscle(s) to balance your strength and coax yourself to better health. Continue to lift weight with less weight on the sore muscle and go through the motion(s) for biofeedback.

When we think of self-improvement plans, we think linear. We think of nice straight lines from where we are at now to our goal. This is a very linear self-improvement plan. Yet you will have your ups and downs due to life.

You are not likely to make it from here to anywhere without setbacks. Some setbacks will be completely out of your control. Most setbacks will be detours and not stops that will involve problem solving. Keep training. Keep going on days when you feel "off"—champions and finishers both do.

Don't fight a fever. The high cost of a fever.

If you run a fever, that is a setback. While I believe training and getting your body temperature up above a hundred degrees is a like self-induced fever that helps the body, a fever from a virus or bacteria really tears down your muscle strength.

For every day you have a fever, your training will be affected for one week. It is important to "break" a fever quickly. Having a fever for four days means that your training will be off for four weeks.

Don't inhale phlegm.

If you have a head or chest cold, heavy inhaling will just drive the fluids and infection deeper into your lungs. If you are not running a fever, yet are very congested, lifting weights or stretching is OK. Spin class is not OK if you are congested and coughing. Don't develop low-level pneumonia by doing hard aerobic training when there are fluids already present in your head and chest.

Training prevents colds and flu.

I really do think aerobic training prevents colds and flu. Taking a daily chlorinated swim probably kills surface bacteria and viruses. Creating a self-induced temperature while you are exercising may fight low-grade infections. Creating mucous and the like with swimming, biking and running probably prevents congestive problems by clearing your sinuses.

If sick or injured, still set aside the time.

Become an expert in what ails you and remain active if you become injured or get sick.

If you can't run because of injury, yet you can still walk comfortably, walk during the run portion of the program. "Walking it off" used to be the cure before more sophisticated physical therapies were developed.

If you can't bike, still keep the routine and set aside that time for other active exercise. Going forwards and backwards on an elliptical trainer is an excellent replacement when you cannot ride. When you go backwards you strengthen your knees by working antagonistic muscles.

If you can't swim, yet you can walk in the water, continue walking exercises in the pool.

If you are so sick or injured you can't do anything, stay in bed when you would normally be training. But keep your routine. Do not let other activities intrude upon your training time. During your training time while resting, visualize and plan on your return to training and racing.

People tend to over invest their money when starting a new enterprise. It's easy to buy the first thing you see because you want to get started right away. These are my suggestions to help you keep your costs down. Following this advice, your equipment will be good enough until you know what works better for you.

Swimming goggles and suit suggestions.

I find Aqua Sphere Kaimen® goggles the single best goggle readily available. These goggles fit about eighty percent of my students comfortably. Because nose and eye shapes differ, goggles are hard to fit. Try on your goggles in the store. Goggles that feel airtight have some suction, even without water around them. Don't make your goggles airtight by tightening the straps. The best fitting goggles fit, with some suction, without even tightening the straps

Good goggles cost about twenty dollars. I used to see Aqua Spheres occasionally at Walmart® for less than fifteen dollars.

Blue tinted lenses are the best color for your indoor and outdoor purposes. Orange is probably the worst color because many triathlon buoys are orange and you can't see the orange for the orange. Orange is also too bright in the morning light. Blue tinted lenses brighten up the indoors and provide a little sun block outdoors.

Goggles that don't work will never allow you to enjoy a swim. Once you find a goggle that you love, always have a second pair on hand.

FINIS® swimwear material is the longest lasting. Long lasting swim material in chlorinated water is a plus. You don't really want to be asking yourself if your drooping suit is still "decent" enough to wear. It would be my wish that swimsuit manufacturers were more competitive in the longevity of their materials in chlorinated water. It would also be helpful if an athletic wear company used swimsuit material to make triathlon shorts.

That said, swimwear is more about fit than long lasting wear—especially for women. Swimwear manufacturers are far behind what women want. Most women would like to buy their tops separate from their bottoms for size. Keeping with one piece suits is like making sport bras dependent on short size.

Biking shoes, shorts and bike suggestions.

I have yet to find a certain brand of cycling shoe that I would steer people to. If the shoe fits great, regardless of the low price or manufacturer, it's the right shoe for you.

The upper part of the shoe ought to feel like a glove and not be too tight. The bottom part of the shoe needs to be solid with no give. If you notice the slightest problem with a shoe, then multiply that problem by 5,000–6,000 steps an hour, before you buy the shoes.

I like several types of cycling shorts, all superior to riding without cycling shorts. This is probably the toughest item to buy in a store and know that it is going to work for you. Over time, you will probably want less padding in the shorts, so keep that in mind when buying. You can even get by with no padding if you can get used to it.

Chamois cream for cycling is also a good idea. It is a cream made of oils, which protects your skin from rash where saddle meets shorts. It goes even further and lasts longer if you apply it to your skin rather than shorts.

I like several brands of bikes, yet most people over invest in the bike. It is tempting to buy speed. Light wheels will make you faster, yet are harder to stay true. Light tires go flat more often. Bike manufacturers really have done a great job on delivering a good product at a low price. The bikes available today are a better value than in the past. To save money, buy your bike with the parts that you want on it. Bikes are relatively inexpensive, while parts and labor are expensive.

A faster bike makes you more competitive in quantifiable ways, as long as you can handle a faster bike. The bike is the "car" of triathlon racing. Compare this to buying a car that you want to learn how to drive with, and buy the race car later.

You can't buy a top three placing at a race when you buy your bike and a faster bike does not make you healthier. Don't over invest in your road bike at this point.

Running shoe suggestions. Lydiard shoe adjustments.

I like shoes with a wide toe box and narrow heel. I wear Nike® shoes with full length air cushioning with a neutral shoe. Cushioning is key. While I would like barefoot running on soft ground through pastures and pine woods, I know it's just not going to happen on a daily basis. Running barefoot is faster and maybe healthier if you can avoid injury. Running barefoot is not practical so seek cushioning, fit and tread wear. Nike wins because their full length air sole lasts longer than the shoe.

Arthur Lydiard had no qualms about modifying shoes with a knife or scissors. There used to be a small piece of fabric above the heel box to hold while pulling on your shoes. That small piece of material would rub your Achilles tendon while running. You would only notice this problem after hours of running. Arthur would have us cut up a brand new pair of shoes rather than injure our Achilles tendon. Today, most manufacturers actually exclude that piece now, and most have a little dip there to avoid the shoe rubbing against the Achilles tendon. The moral is not to take what manufacturers produce as gospel as to what is right for you.

Suggestions for socks and tops.

Walmart® can be a source for some good triathlon wear. Walmart Starter® socks are a wonderful value. I have not found a better performing sock, even for more money. Buy the ones that are 98% Polyester / 2% Spandex. They keep the moisture off your feet and retain their cushion over time.

Walmart Starter ®tops also do a good job of wicking sweat off you. I wish Starter also had real swimwear, cycling shorts or triathlon shorts made out of swimwear material.

Swim while looking backwards and forwards to stay on course.

When you swim outdoors, you will be glad you practiced looking forward while in the pool. Some people can sight forward while maintaining a freestyle stroke. If that does not work for you, sight forward while doing the breaststroke. Another benefit of sighting with the breaststroke is that you will give your freestyle muscles a break. This break could actually have you swimming faster. Look where you want to go often when swimming outdoors. There is nothing so frustrating as swimming off course.

Bike within yourself. Everything is more important than you (cars, people, and potholes).

You could crash if you are not riding within yourself. I have seen riders so tired that they crash while getting on and off their bike. It's common to stop looking ahead or just a few feet in front of your front wheel when you are tired and hit something while riding.

Of course, the answer is to be in better shape. When you are in really good shape, you will be surprised at how much your bike handling skills have improved. Until you are in better shape, ride within yourself and don't be in a hurry to crash.

Run or walk or walk and run to finish.

There is no shame in walking. Remember not to do anything today that will screw up your performance tomorrow. Walking can be much healthier than running if you are approaching exhaustion or injury. If you are running and are wondering if you could walk as fast as you are running, try walking for a while.

Once I won a race by walking a little when I was ahead and out of sight of my competition. Walking can be an effective strategy to finish in order to achieve your goals.

Show up early for the race to lower the anxiety.

You will be nervous on race day. Waiting in long lines for registration or the bathroom will not reduce your nervousness. It's actually much more relaxing to sit down and watch others standing in line. Show up early. It's like being at the front of the race.

Start slow so you don't finish even slower.

Most races are not lost in the middle or the end of a race. Most races are lost in the first minutes of the race. If you want proof, look at a high school track meet race of one or two miles. Seldom is the front runner of the first or second lap the winner. These "rabbits" do themselves in for the benefit of the smarter runners who hold back, waiting for the "rabbits" to tire.

If you want to experience this for yourself when training, immediately start out at a pace you would "dream" of keeping up, and keep going that fast. The following week, start at a pace that is slower than your training pace and very gradually speed it up because you will want to go faster. Compare your times and your emotions. This is a lesson that experience teaches better than I can put in words.

In my first marathon, I wasn't even in the top fifty after six miles. I finished second overall. I passed a lot of rabbits. And there was no way that I would have won if I had started faster. The winner was over six minutes faster and I was spent running my first marathon in 2:48. Yet starting slower than better collegiate runners gave me an emotional and physical boost when I passed them.

Your goal is to feel that you are gradually going faster.

Your goal is to feel that you are gradually going faster and getting healthier. If you go out too fast, you will really doubt your training and yourself.

Your aerobic threshold is easy to determine.

You can go fast aerobically, eventually. Marathoners run faster than a four minute and fifty second pace per mile for over two hours. That's aerobic. When your body is not producing lactic acid, you are training and racing aerobically.

Anaerobic training can be felt pretty fast and is limited. A person can't go more than fifteen minutes anaerobically. If you are cycling or running anaerobically, you feel what they call a "burn". This burning sensation is your muscles trying to accomplish chemically what it can no longer do aerobically. Children can keep the burn going o on much longer than older adults. Older adults need to respect the "burn" because anaerobic production is limited. Aerobic production is unlimited.

When you are training or racing, approach the burn point, yet never go into that burning sensation. The problem with going into the burn is that when you recover from the burn, your body slows down even further in aerobic mode to satisfy current aerobic needs and get rid of the chemical burn.

With the finish line in sight, you can go "all out", if you want.

Finally the finish line is in sight. You can go all out if you want. If you get the "burn", you can walk it off after the race. The remainder of today and tomorrow will be recovery time.

Measuring adaptation and progression in the smallest increments.

Your progress is at the cellular level. Your capillaries won't suddenly grow because you sprint or run up a steep hill. Most people don't have the patience to find out how good they can be because they don't realize that it's their cells that are changing.

It's not as simple as your lungs or heart or muscles getting bigger or stronger. Your lung capacity doesn't change as much as you might think. You actually change your blood at the cellular level to carry more oxygen and fuel to the muscle. At the cellular level, the body grows capillaries that distribute oxygen and fuel better to the muscle. Think of a tree's root system. The tree's growth depends on its roots; what you can't see happening under the surface.

If your physical development is at the cellular level, it's a mistake to use large measures like minutes to measure your weekly progress. Even the smallest unit that you are capable of measuring is probably bigger than the cellular rate of change.

Because you are measuring your progress with your weekly run, be thrilled as long as you run .01 miles or seventeen yards further over twenty minutes. True, you won't get to the Olympics this year or in four years from now at that rate. Yet, Olympians and their ancestors have been changing themselves at the cellular level for a very long time. In this one way, life is fair. One year of training is not going beat five years of training.

You improve at the cellular level.

The Indoor Triathlete Program is all about changing you, aerobically, at the cellular level. With cellular respiration, your aerobic function is nineteen times more effective than your anaerobic function.

Red blood cells live about 120 days and your body produces new ones. You need to coax the body aerobically with stress to develop new and improved red blood cells. Red blood cells carry oxygen and fuel to the muscles. When you improve your red blood cells your lungs, heart and muscles receive the benefit.

Also, you probably don't have the nerve endings firing at the cellular level as fast or as powerfully as you would like. Improvement in the firing of synapses will also come with training.

Hopefully, this knowledge about yourself will give you a long-term approach to your training, health and fitness. It's been said that the body replaces most of it cells within a seven-year period. And from my experience, you really won't find out just how good you can be until you are five to ten years into your transformation.

Nerve, arteriole and capillary development is the key.

Keep the pressure up, blood pressure that is, to grow arterioles and capillaries in your muscles. A higher blood pressure while training is necessary to develop your "root" system. If you let your blood pressure drop for more than fifteen seconds every fifteen minutes, you won't develop the arterioles and capillaries optimally. Arthur would let us get a drink while running, yet we couldn't stand around the store talking about how hard the training was.

While you are transitioning from bike to run to swim, don't rest. Keep moving to keep your blood pressure up. While training and racing, "rest" by going slower. Avoid rest that is a complete stop for more than fifteen seconds each fifteen minutes. If anything, during the transitions you may notice your heart rate go up. Hurrying from one activity to the next does keep up the blood pressure promoting the cellular growth you want.

Also consider the cellular level of your nervous system. If you have an injury where the nerves die, the nerves grow back. If you are teaching yourself new movements, you have to learn the movements physically, not just in your head, and your nerve cells need to learn the movement and "fire" appropriately.

While your cells are changing, focus on more mindful activity, like technique and calculating your pace.

The moment you feel injury, back off and stop.

As I said earlier, the best coaches will know when to hold you back. If you are biking or running or swimming or weightlifting and have an "Oh, no" moment, stop as soon as you can. You will be better off two days from now when the program has you back on the bike or run if you stop before you repetitively traumatize the area. Do not repetitively traumatize anything. Triathlon gains come from consistent aerobic gains, not pain.

To improve, learn to understand each event better.

You will probably never have your swim perfected technically due to the changing nature of your body. You can take that as a positive and be glad that you will always have something to work on to improve.

Swimming needs size or high stroke rate and good technique.

Swimming requires MOMENTUM. MOMENTUM = MASS x VELOCITY.

On one side are big swimmers that do well taking fewer strokes because they have MASS and their momentum does not drop as much in between swim strokes.

On the other side are small swimmers that do well taking many strokes with shorter arms; they create VELOCITY because their momentum, without much mass, drops relatively fast in between strokes.

A good swim coach will coach you properly. Regardless of your size, swimming is very technical and it is helpful to have a good coach that will orient you to breathing, positioning your weight, and building a swim stroke that is right for your size.

Cycling needs time and equipment.

The best cyclists in the world spend hours on the bike conditioning. You will be no different. As you get used to the schedule, add more time to the bike. You will notice the benefit of even five to ten minutes more.

Arthur often said, "Miles make the champions". Arthur applied this in many ways. Running another mile was more helpful to running than any other activity. Your time on the bike will help your bike riding more than any of the other activities in this program. I am also using the time on the bike to offset the wear and tear of the run.

After you have become comfortable with your initial investment, it is normal to want better equipment. You may want better brakes because you are now going faster. A year from now, you will know more about cycling equipment, so spend some time obtaining information before you invest more money in replacing what is good enough now.

Running needs legs.

Save your legs in training and racing. Some of you may be coming to this program with sore, tired or even injured legs. As I have said, you can always walk. Walking is healthy exercise and I am sure that you would like to be able to walk as long as you are alive.

If your legs are just fine, keep them that way by picking up your heels and float while you are running. Get good again at lifting and landing. Don't worry about foot placement because if you never really lift your leg, foot placement becomes less relevant. If you lift your feet and legs behind you, you will go faster than if you focus on foot plant.

The best athlete in your high school today could be you.

The first "Rocky" story was outstanding. Rocky's goal of being the first person left standing at the end of the fight is much like your story.

Training indoors is not like training outdoors on the island of Maui, site of the Hawaii Ironman. Training indoors is "good enough" though. Like Rocky punching the sides of beef in the meat locker, you can train indoors consistently and become the best athlete in your high school today.

Good luck and keep me posted on your progress.

Sincerely,

Bill Hammons, The Indoor Triathlete.

Appendix A – Sprint Triathlon Relative Swim, Bike, Run Comparisons

Average Run Mile 5K	Average Swim Pace 100 yards	Average Bike MPH 12.4 miles	Estimated Time without transitions
5:00	**1:20**	**24**	**52:00**
6:00	1:40	22	59:00
7:00	2:00	20	1:07:00
8:00	2:20	18	1:16:00
9:00	2:40	16	1:25:00
10:00	**3:00**	**14**	**1:36:00**
11:00	3:20	12	1:49:00
12:00	3:40	11	2:00:00
13:00	4:00	10	2:11:00

Easy to remember numbers, based on my perception of effort across the three events. I purposely kept these numbers rounded for ease of use and accuracy. There are so many factors in each case that rounding may add to their accuracy.

Remember that the chart above is your average minutes per mile pace for over 3.1 miles; your hundred yard swim pace for four hundred yards and your miles per hour on the bike for 12.4 miles. If you can swim one hundred yards in a minute twenty seconds don't assume that you can swim that pace for 400 yards (neither can I), or run a five minute mile, and bike twenty-four miles an hour in a triathlon.

Translating   5:00   1:20   24   52:00
A great athlete, with strengths in all three events, could average a minute twenty seconds for a 400 yard swim for a total time of 5:20. After the swim, hop on the bike and average 24mph for 12.4 miles for 31 minutes and then run a 5K at a 5:00 pace for 15:32 minutes. Total time without transitions would be around fifty-two minutes. Including the transition times from the swim to the bike and then off bike and running, total sprint time would be at world record level in the area of fifty four minutes.

Translating   10:00   3:00   14   1:36:00
A good result, depending on the person, could be a 12 minute swim, a bike of 53 minutes and a run of 31 minutes for a total time of an hour and thirty six minutes without transitions. With transitions, in the area of an hour and forty minutes for a sprint triathlon.

Appendix B – Indoor Triathlete Club, a national USAT club

If you want ongoing feedback and information, there is a USAT club that I created as a national, on line triathlon club.

The website is www.indoortriathlete.com and I give on going advice to triathletes who have joined the club. You can log your training on a spreadsheet for comparisons; enter discussions and ask me questions; and keep current with my training recommendations.

Joining the club would be a good way for us to keep up with one another.

www.ingramcontent.com/pod-product-compliance
Lightning Source LLC
Chambersburg PA
CBHW071021040426

42443CB00007B/886